Informatica PR000007 Questions & Dumps

Exam Prep Questions for PR000007 latest version

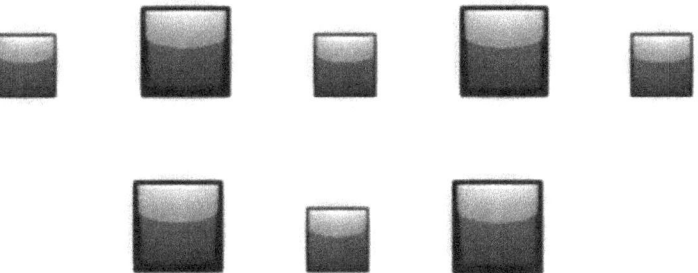

Authored By: Maxim Books

Copyright Notice © 2023 – Maxim Books

Protected by copyright law. No piece of this distribution might be repeated, distributed, or sent in any structure or using any and all means, including copying, recording, or other electronic or robotized strategies, without the earlier composed assent of the distributor, with the exception of brief citations exemplified in basic audits and certain other noncommercial purposes allowed by intellectual property owner.

About Maxim Books:

Maxim Books is a book publishing company incorporated in Dallas, Texas, USA, a place that is accessible both on the web and locally, which releases the force of education substances, Certifications guidebooks, poetry, and numerous other book genres. We make it simple for authors and writers to get their books planned, distributed, marketed, and sell expertly on an international scale with digital book + Print conveyance. Maxim Books was established in 2018 and expanding its business in more countries

Note: Answers of the questions are at the end of the book

QUESTION 1
When copying and replacing folders in PowerCenter version 9.10 , which of the following statements is true?

A. The move is performed in two steps. The first step involves copying the source folder contents Into temp tables. At this point the target repository is in a read-only mode. The second step involves moving the information from the temp tables into the target folder. During this step the repository is locked.
B. The move is performed in one step. This involves copying the source folder contents into the target folder. During this step the repository is locked.
C. The move is performed in two steps. The first step involves copying the source folder contents into XML files. The second step involves importing the XML files into the target folder. During this step the repository is locked.
D. The Source Folder is copied Into the target folder. No locks are placed on the target repository.

QUESTION 2
What are the three basic security objects that are created and maintained in the Security tab of the Informatica Administrator?

A. Users, Groups. Permissions
B. Users, Groups, Privileges
C. Users, Groups, Roles
D. Users, Groups, Folders

QUESTION 3
Which statement best describes the relationship between system roles and custom roles?

A. System roles cannot be edited and custom roles can be edited.

B. A custom role is created by editing a system role.
C. A custom role is created by copying a system role, renaming it and editing at least one of the privileges.
D. Any number of custom roles can be created within each system role.

QUESTION 4
Which answer below correctly describes the process to add a new node to an existing domain?

A. Use the Informatica installer to install the Service Manager on the new node. Joining it to the existing domain.
B. Use the Informatica installer to create a new domain with the new node. Then use the Informatica Administrator to join the new domain with the existing domain.
C. Use the Informatica Administration create the new node. Then use the Actions menu to start the Service Manager on the new node.
D. You must first shut down the domain and then use the infa setup command to add the node.

QUESTION 5
You enter the user name Administrator as the required Domain Administrator user during the installation of a new Informatica domain.

What is the result?

A. This action is not permitted because the user Administrator is already built into the domain. You must supply another user name to be the Domain Administrator.
B. The Domain Administrator becomes the default Administrator. The password you assign to the Domain Administrator is assigned to the default Administrator.

C. The Domain Administrator becomes the default Administrator, but you must supply the current Administrator password or the Installation cannot proceed.
D. Two users named Administrator now exist, one of which is a Domain Administrator (with the password you supply) and the other is the default Administrator super user with the default password.

QUESTION 6
What is best practice when using the folder copy method to deploy metadata? Assume for this question:

1. Objects in the shortcut folder and the folder that is to be copied have both been modified
2. Objects in the shortcut folder are referenced by objects in the folder you wish to deploy

A. Copy the shortcut folder first, then the folder that you wish to deploy.
B. Copy the folder you wish to deploy first, then the shortcut folder.
C. You may safely ignore the shortcut folder and only copy the folder you wish to deploy.
D. Copy the shortcut folder with Repository Manager and the other folders with Workflow Manager.

QUESTION 7
Which statement best describes the process when a user connects to a PowerCenter Repository Service for the first time?

Assume the following:

A. The user connects directly and immediately to the Repository service.

B. The user connects to the service manager of the gateway node, and after authentication and authorization, is reassigned to the Repository Service.
C. The user connects to the service manager of the worker node that is running the Repository service, is then authenticated, authorized, and connected to the PowerCenter Repository service.
D. The user first connects to the PowerCenter Integration Service and then after authentication and authorization, is connected to the PowerCenter Repository Service.

QUESTION 8
Which connection types are allowed for the Informatica Administrator interface?

A. HTTPS
B. HTTP or HTTPS
C. HTTPS or LDAP
D. Native or LDAP

QUESTION 9
Which of the following permissions can be associated with a PowerCenter repository folder?

A. Grant
B. Execute
C. Create global objects
D. Create runtime objects

QUESTION 10
Why should you use PowerCenter Metadata Exchange (MX) views rather than querying the PowerCenter repository tables directly- i.e. the ones that begin with OPB_?

A. Querying the PowerCenter repository tables directly is a violation of the PowerCenter license and terms of use.
B. PowerConter repository tables store most data in proprietary binary format and hence are not directly readable. This binary format improves performance.
C. Stored (hard-coded) queries against the repository tables may become invalid upon a repository version upgrade due to the fact that the repository table structures may change.
D. It is not possible to query the repository tables directly.

QUESTION 11
How many different repository services can be associated with a single integration service?

A. One
B. One or more
C. Zero or more
D. One if the integration service is not part of a grid, more than one if It is part of a grid

QUESTION 12
Which application(s) can be used to copy a PowerCenter repository folder?

A. The Repository Manager.
B. The Repository Manager or the Informatica Administrator.
C. The Repository Manager or the Designer.
D. Any application except the Workflow Monitor.

QUESTION 13
When using pmrep to import objects from XML which choice would be following best practice?

A. Run pmrep In Interactive mode so each conflict can be answered directly.
B. Use a control file.
C. Use a shell script or batch file.
D. Import the objects manually instead of using pmrep so the conflicts can be handled in the XML import wizard.

QUESTION 14
Which statement below best describes how to change a worker node to a gateway node?

A. By changing a property of the node.
B. By changing a property of the node and the domain.
C. By changing a property of the node and setting each service that runs on that node to Primary node
D. By reinstalling the Service Manager on that node and configuring it to run as a gateway node.

QUESTION 15
Complete this sentence Each operating system profile can have a different _?

A. Integration Service
B. Node
C. Process variable root directory
D. Log agent

QUESTION 16
What is the purpose of operating system profiles?

A. To allow two or more workflows to run on the same node under different operating system users.
B. To allow two or more Integration Services to run on the same node under differed operating system users.

C. To allow two or more workflows to run on the same node while accessing different database connection users.
D. To allow two or more Integration Services to run a single workflow on two or more different nodes with different operating systems.

QUESTION 17
Which statement is true regarding object copy across folders in the Repository Manager?

A. You can copy an object even though it has been checked out or has a write-intent lock.
B. The Repository service will lock the repository database until the objects have been copied.
C. It is best practice to export the objects as XML prior to performing the copy operation.
D. You must have write permissions in both the origin folder and the destination folder.

QUESTION 18
In reference to relational connections created in the PowerCenter Workflow Manager, which one of the following statements is true?

A. The connection environment SQL executes when a session connects to the database.
B. The transaction environment SQL executes Just before a COMMIT against the target.
C. The transaction environment SQL causes PowerCenter to ignore the Transaction Control Transformation.
D. You can use the connection environment SQL to set folder permissions in the PowerCenter repository database.

QUESTION 19
Pmcmd is used for which of the following tasks?

A. Delete workflow, schedule workflow, ping service.
B. Start workflow, schedule workflow, ping service.
C. Start workflow, delete task, ping service.
D. Start workflow, schedule workflow, copy workflow.

QUESTION 20
Why would a repository service be placed in Exclusive mode?

A. If the repository service will be the only service running on a node.
B. If the repository service is not to be configured to run in backup mode.
C. In order to change a property of the repository service.
D. If it is desired to prevent the repository service from running as part of a grid.

QUESTION 21
In Informatics 9.x, which is true about domain configuration backup using the infasetup command line program'?

A. It Backs up the domain database and all service databases that are part of that domain.
B. It backs up domain metadata to another domain database.
C. It backs up the domain configuration to a binary file.
D. It backs up the domain to two binary files, one of which holds an index and the other the data.

QUESTION 22
Infacmd is used to administer which of the following objects?

A. Domain gateway, log events, workflows, application services.
B. Versioning. log events, grids, application services.
C. Domain gateway, log events, grids, application services.
D. Domain gateway, clients, grids, application services.

QUESTION 23
What is the difference between the Default Administrator and the Domain Administrator users'?

A. The Default Administrator is automatically created during installation. Domain Administrators must be created manually.
B. The Domain Administrator is automatically created for all domains, and the Default Administrator must be created during the domain installation process.
C. The Default Administrator is user supplied during the installation process, and the Domain Administrator Is the built-in super user for everyday domain administration.
D. Both users are automatically created in all domains, but the Domain Administrator is used to maintain only domain objects, while the Default Administrator can be used to manage any Informatica object including clients.

QUESTION 24
You have coped a set of PowerCenter objects to a new folder, Many of the objects that now appear in the destination folder have a "1" appended to their names, such as 'Targetname1 instead of the expected Targetname.

How would you recommend avoiding this situation in the future"?

A. Delete duplicate objects in the destination folder prior to copying.
B. Rename duplicate objects In the destination folder prior to copying.
C. Resolve duplicate conflicts with "replace" or "reuse." Resolve duplicate conflicts with "rename" and manually provide an alternate name for the object.

QUESTION 25
You are migrating a domain to a new domain database.

What is the correct order of the next actions to complete the migration once the new domain database is successfully restored?

A. Start all nodes, update database configuration on each node, enable application services.
B. Update database configuration on each node, start all nodes, enable application services.
C. Enable application services, start all nodes, update database configuration on each node.
D. Start all nodes, enable application services, update database configuration on each node.

QUESTION 26
To run a pmcmd command line command and then confirm the command has run successfully, which method would be used?

A. Read the return code visually or in a shell script or batch file.
B. Check the status of the command in the Workflow Monitor.

C. Run the command from the informatica Administrator and check the status after the command has completed.
D. Create and configure an Email alert within the workflow Monitor.

QUESTION 27
How are license keys obtained for Informatica products?

A. As a separate download.
B. Encoded on the install CD.
C. License keys can be generated on-site using the mfasetup.sh script.
D. License keys can be generated on-site using your product code and the informatica Administrator.

QUESTION 28
A customer has purchased license keys for nodes running both the Windows and UNIX operating systems Can they run one Windows node and one UNIX node?

A. Yes provided the nodes are in different domains.
B. Yes, if both nodes are within the same domain.
C. Yes, but this arrangement requires a PowerCenter Grid license to be activated.
D. Yes, but a primary service on one of the nodes cannot be configured to run as a backup service on the other node.

QUESTION 29
When creating a repository folder what does the Allow Shortcut option provide?

A. Objects in the folder can be created more quickly.
B. Metadata shortcuts will be allowed within this folder.

C. Metadata shortcuts will be allowed across repositories even if they are not in the same repository domain.
D. Shortcuts created in other folders may reference metadata from this folder.

QUESTION 30
The Informatica Administrator can configure an automatic email alert to notify failure of which types of objects? Assume that service process failover is in effect.

A. Nodes, integration services, repository services.
B. Nodes and any domain service.
C. Nodes, integration services, repository services, workflows.
D. Nodes, any domain service, workflows.

QUESTION 31
A node has been selected in the Informatica Administrator Domain Navigator window. The Processes tab for this node contains which of the following items?

A. All of the service processes and their statuses.
B. All of the workflows running on the node.
C. All of the service processes running on the node that are disabled.
D. All of the service processes running on the node that are enabled.

QUESTION 32
Which statement best describes the characteristics of system-defined roles?

A. Created by Administrator, cannot be edited or deleted.

B. Created by Informatica, may be edited or deleted by Administrator.
C. Created by informatica, cannot be edited or deleted by Administrator.
D. Created by Administrator, may be edited or deleted by Administrator.

QUESTION 33
What is the purpose of a Repository Service?

A. To run PowerCenter Workflows.
B. To run and schedule PowerCenter workflows, validate mappings.
C. To manage PowerCenter, Data Quality and Web Services metadata objects.
D. To manage PowerCenter metadata objects.

QUESTION 34
Infasetup is used for which of the following tasks?

A. Create domain, restore domain, define repository service.
B. Backup domain, restore domain, update gateway node.
C. Backup domain, copy domain, define integration service.
D. Backup domain, restore domain, define integration service.

QUESTION 35
Which statement is true about Roles in Informatica?

A. Roles may not contain any Privileges.
B. Roles may only be assigned to Users.

C. Roles are a collection of one or more privileges.
D. Roles may only be assigned to users in a native domain.

QUESTION 36
When creating a new repository service, a database username (schema) must be specified to hold the metadata tables

Can the new repository service use a database schema that contains existing repository tables and objects? Assume you need to preserve the existing objects.

A. No. For a new repository service, the database schema must be empty.
B. No. When the new service is created, existing tables will be automatically dropped.
C. Yes. The tables and objects will be preserved by default.
D. Yes. The user must select the creation option, "Do not create new content.

QUESTION 37
With respect to license keys used in the Informatica domain, choose the answer below that is correct

A. Each license key object can have only one license key.
B. Each license key object can have multiple license keys.
C. Each service can be associated with multiple license keys.
D. One license key object is used for the domain, and it can have multiple keys associated with it.

QUESTION 38
If a domain contains only two nodes, which configuration below is not allowed?

A. Both nodes are gateway nodes at the same time, with Informatica automatically deciding which is the master gateway when the domain is started.
B. Both nodes are worker nodes at the same time.
C. One node or a master gateway, the other is a worker.
D. Only one node is active and it is the master gateway node.

QUESTION 39
The Informatica Administrator can be used to do all of these actions except for which one?

A. To create a domain.
B. To shut down a domain.
C. To create a service.
D. To apply a different license key to a service.

QUESTION 40
A Model Repository Service is associated with what Informatica product?

A. Power center
B. Data Quality
C. Both Power center and Data Quality
D. Both Data Quality and Metadata Reporting

QUESTION 41
You need to create 60 Informatica Domain users.

You wish to assign them the same privileges without having to specify the privileges for each individual user.

What is your recommended approach?

A. Place all the users in the same domain folder and set privileges on the folder.
B. Place all the users in the same group and set privileges on the group.
C. Create a role with the desired privileges and grant each user that role.
D. Use LDAP In conjunction with a domain folder organized with the desired privileges.

QUESTION 42
Which of the following statements is true in reference to License Keys?

A. A license key may be assigned to a Repository Service running in normal mode.
B. A license key may be assigned to a Repository Service running in exclusive mode.
C. A license key may be assigned to a Repository Service that is disabled
D. A license key may only be assigned to a service at install time.

QUESTION 43
PowerCenter Web Service Hubs use which one of the following?

A. The SOAP standard and a fixed XML data structure to receive requests and send responses to web service clients.
B. The RPC (Remote Procedure Call) standard to receive requests and send responses to web service clients.
C. The soap standard to receive requests and send responses to web service clients.

D. The rpc (Remote Procedure call) standard and a fixed XML data structure to receive requests and send ^responses to web service clients.

QUESTION 44
Which is the best PowerCenter client application to use to copy a workflow into an empty folder in a different repository?

A. The Workflow Manager, because the destination folder is empty.
B. The Workflow Manager, because only one workflow is to be transferred.
C. The Repository Manager, because It is the only client application that can transfer objects between repositories.
D. The Repository Manager, because it will automatically associate the correct mapping with the sessions in the workflow.

QUESTION 45
You can create PowerCenter connection objects within which client tool(s)?

A. Workflow Manager
B. Workflow Manager or Workflow Monitor
C. Workflow Manager or Repository Manager
D. Repository Manager or Informatica Administrator

QUESTION 46
Which of the following statements is true about running a PowerCenter workflow?
A. The Data Transformation Manager (DTM) process starts and locks the workflow and runs the workflow tasks.

B. The PowerCenter Integration Service process starts and locks the workflow and runs the workflow tasks.
C. The Data Transformation Manager (DTM) process starts the PowerCenter Integration Service process to run each Session and Command task within a workflow.
D. PowerCenter Invokes the Data Transformation Manager (DTM) only when the developer saves a mapping.

QUESTION 47
Which command line tool is used to create Informatica user accounts?

A. pmcep
B. infacmd
C. infasetup
D. pmcmd

QUESTION 48
Which step(s) must be followed to make a copy of the PowerCenter repository metadata? Assume that the source repository is in a separate domain from the new repository.

A. Backup the source repository to a file 2. Create a Repository Service for the new repository that has no tables 3. Restore the backup file to the new repository
B. Backup the source repository to a file 2. Create a Repository Service for the new repository that has tables 3. Restore the backup file to the new repository
C. Use the "Copy Contents" feature in the Administrator Tool
D. Create a Repository Service for the new repository that has no tables 2. In the Repository Manager Tool, click and drag the source repository to the new repository

QUESTION 49
When is it advisable to migrate PowerCenter repository objects between domains using the XML export- import method?

A. When the master gateway node on the domains are running on different operating systems.
B. When the domain databases are in different database types (Oracle and Sybase, for example).
C. When the PowerCenter Repository Manager cannot access the repositories in both domains at the same time.
D. When the license key for Team Based Development - Deployment Groups is not available.

QUESTION 50
Complete the following sentence A process variable root directory is associated with a _?

A. Node
B. Integration service
C. Repository service
D. Domain

QUESTION 51
Which of the following services does not require a database connection as part of its configuration?

A. The Powercenter Repository service.
B. The Powercenter Integration Service.
C. The PowerCenter Designer Service.
D. The Reporting Service.

QUESTION 52
Where does Informatica 9.1 store encrypted passwords?

A. Domain Configuration database
B. PowerCenter Repository database
C. Domain Security database
D. Service Manager Repository

QUESTION 53
Which object below can be imported into a domain from LDAP?

A. Permissions
B. Privileges
C. Groups
D. Roles

QUESTION 54
What may be gained when registering more than one Integration Service to a single Repository Service?

A. Performance
B. Reliability
C. Redundancy to facilitate automatic failover
D. Ability to partition the sessions, assuming the partition license option has been purchased

QUESTION 55
Which method would you use to migrate objects (such as a workflow) from a development repository to a production repository, if both repositories cannot be accessed from the same Repository Manager?

A. XML export-import

B. Object copy
C. Folder copy
D. Deployment group copy

QUESTION 56
Which operations can be done with an incremental key?

A. Add functionality, delete functionality.
B. Add functionality, delete functionality, extend expiration date.
C. Add functionality, delete functionality, enable additional services.
D. Add functionality, delete functionality, enable additional services, extend expiration date.

QUESTION 57
Which PowerCenter application(s) can be used to start a workflow?

A. The Workflow Manager.
B. The Workflow Monitor.
C. The Workflow Manager or the Workflow Monitor.
D. The Workflow Manager, the Workflow Monitor, or the Informatica Administrator.

QUESTION 58
What factors must be considered to import an object stored as XML into a repository?

A. The user who created the original object.
B. The privileges and permissions on the original object.
C. The PowerCenter version or dot-version of the original object.

D. The PowerCenter version or dot-version of the original object, and the privileges and permissions on the original object.

QUESTION 59
Which of the following can be configured as the security protocol used for Domain Management?

A. SFTP (Secure File Transfer Protocol) or SSL (Secure Sockets Layer)
B. TCP/IP (Internet Protocol Suite) or TLS (Transport Layer Security)
C. SSH (Secure Shell) or SSL (Secure Sockets Layer)
D. SSL (Secure Sockets Layer) or TLS (Transport Layer Security)

QUESTION 60
Which of the following is true about PowerCenter Repositories and Integration Services?

A. An Integration Service may be connected to more than one Repository Service.
B. An Integration Service may be connected to only one Repository Service.
C. Repository Service is a client of an Integration Service.
D. A Repository Service may be connected to more than one Integration Service and an Integration Service may be connected to more than one Repository Service.

QUESTION 61
If a user is denied read permission on a folder, which of the following is true?

A. The folder is not visible in the Navigator window in any PowerCenter client.
B. The folder becomes a shared folder.

C. The folder has a red "X" over it.
D. The folder is grayed out in the Navigator window for any PowerCenter client.

QUESTION 62
Which is a type of connection object you can create with PowerCenter?

A. FTP
B. TCP/IP
C. Partitioned
D. Dynamic database

QUESTION 63
What needs to be done to inherit domain privileges"

A. Use domain folders.
B. Use domain groups.
C. Set the privileges on a set-vice level.
D. Set the privileges on a service or group level.

QUESTION 64
When copying a folder across repositories, which statement is true?

A. The origin repository is locked part of the time during the transfer.
B. The destination repository is locked part of the time during the transfer.
C. PowerCenter will automatically create and delete XML files to facilitate transferring the objects.
D. The origin folder must first be exported as XML.

QUESTION 65
The Service Manager runs which functions on the Master Gateway Node in the domain?

A. Workflows, Configuration, and Alerting.
B. Security, Web Services, and Alerting.
C. Security, Configuration, and Alerting.
D. Web Services, Configuration, and Licensing.

QUESTION 66
If you attempt to delete a user who is the owner of a repository folder, what will happen?

A. The folder is deleted.
B. The folder becomes owned by Administrator.
C. You will be prompted to assign another owner to the folder.
D. This operation is not allowed.

QUESTION 67
What is the PowerCenter Data Transformation Manager process used for'?

A. To manage PowerCenter transformation metadata.
B. To spawn threads that run the sessions and workflows.
C. To dynamically balance the loads of workflows and sessions running in parallel.
D. To allocate memory to all running ETL transformations to ensure efficiency.

QUESTION 68
Which PowerCenter service actually runs workflows?

A. Repository service.

B. Integration service.
C. DTM service.
D. Both an Integration service and a Data Integration service.

QUESTION 69
Select the correct statement below regarding nodes

A. Each node must have a hostname set as a property of the node.
B. A minimum of two nodes are required for a running domain, one gateway node and one worker node.
C. Each node is running a service manager for each service on the node.
D. When a gateway node fails, the domain will shut down.

QUESTION 70
Which kinds of objects are stored in a PowerCenter Repository?

A. Mapping objects, sources and targets, workflow objects, operating system semaphores.
B. Mapping objects, sources and targets, workflow objects, workflow run information.
C. Source data, sources and targets, workflow objects, workflow run information.
D. Mapping objects, target data, workflow objects, workflow tasks.

Answers

1. Correct Answer: D

2. Correct Answer: C

3. Correct Answer: A

4. Correct Answer: C

5. Correct Answer: D

6. Correct Answer: C

7. Correct Answer: C

8. Correct Answer: B

9. Correct Answer: B

10. Correct Answer: B

11. Correct Answer: A

12. Correct Answer: B

13. Correct Answer: B

14. Correct Answer: A

15. Correct Answer: C

16. Correct Answer: D

17. Correct Answer: B

18. Correct Answer: A

19. Correct Answer: B

20. Correct Answer: C

21. Correct Answer: C

22. Correct Answer: D

23. Correct Answer: A

24. Correct Answer: B

25. Correct Answer: D

26. Correct Answer: B

27. Correct Answer: A

28. Correct Answer: B

29. Correct Answer: C

30. Correct Answer: A

31. Correct Answer: D

32. Correct Answer: C

33. Correct Answer: B

34. Correct Answer: B

35. Correct Answer: C

36. Correct Answer: C

37. Correct Answer: C

38. Correct Answer: A

39. Correct Answer: D

40. Correct Answer: C

41. Correct Answer: D

42. Correct Answer: A

43. Correct Answer: C

44. Correct Answer: A

45. Correct Answer: A

46. Correct Answer: B

47. Correct Answer: B

48. Correct Answer: A

49. Correct Answer: B

50. Correct Answer: C

51. Correct Answer: C

52. Correct Answer: B

53. Correct Answer: C

54. Correct Answer: A

55. Correct Answer: D

56. Correct Answer: C

57. Correct Answer: A

58. Correct Answer: B

59. Correct Answer: A

60. Correct Answer: C

61. Correct Answer: D

62. Correct Answer: A

63. Correct Answer: B

64. Correct Answer: B

65. Correct Answer: D

66. Correct Answer: B

67. Correct Answer: A

68. Correct Answer: B

69. Correct Answer: C

70. Correct Answer: B

www.ingramcontent.com/pod-product-compliance
Lightning Source LLC
Chambersburg PA
CBHW080438220526
45465CB00009B/3331